A is for Ace

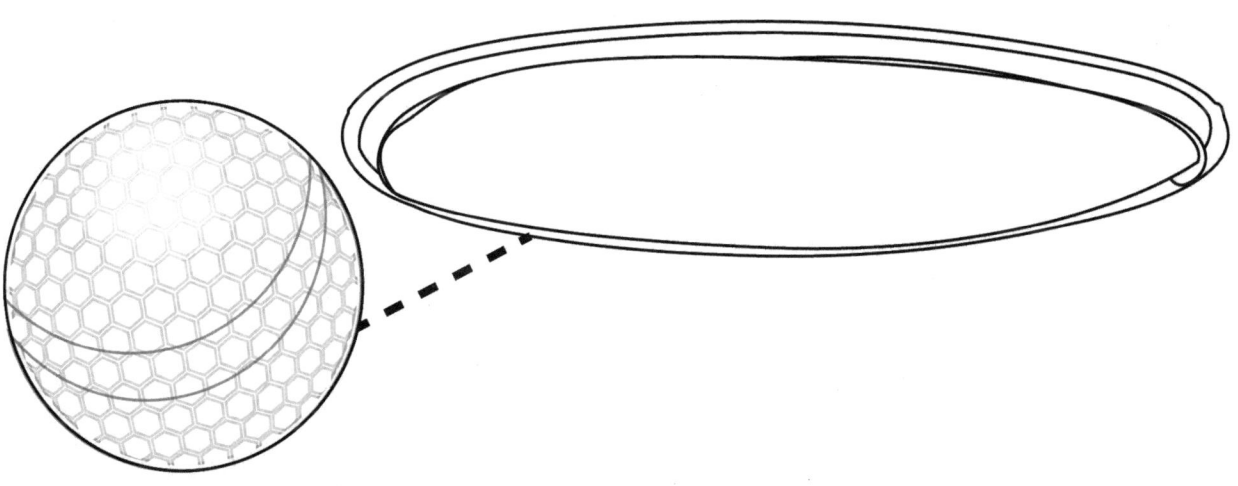

A great shot that's fun

B is for Ball

That we hit on the run

C is for Cart

With tires that spin

D is for Driver

A club we hit with a grin

E is for Eagle

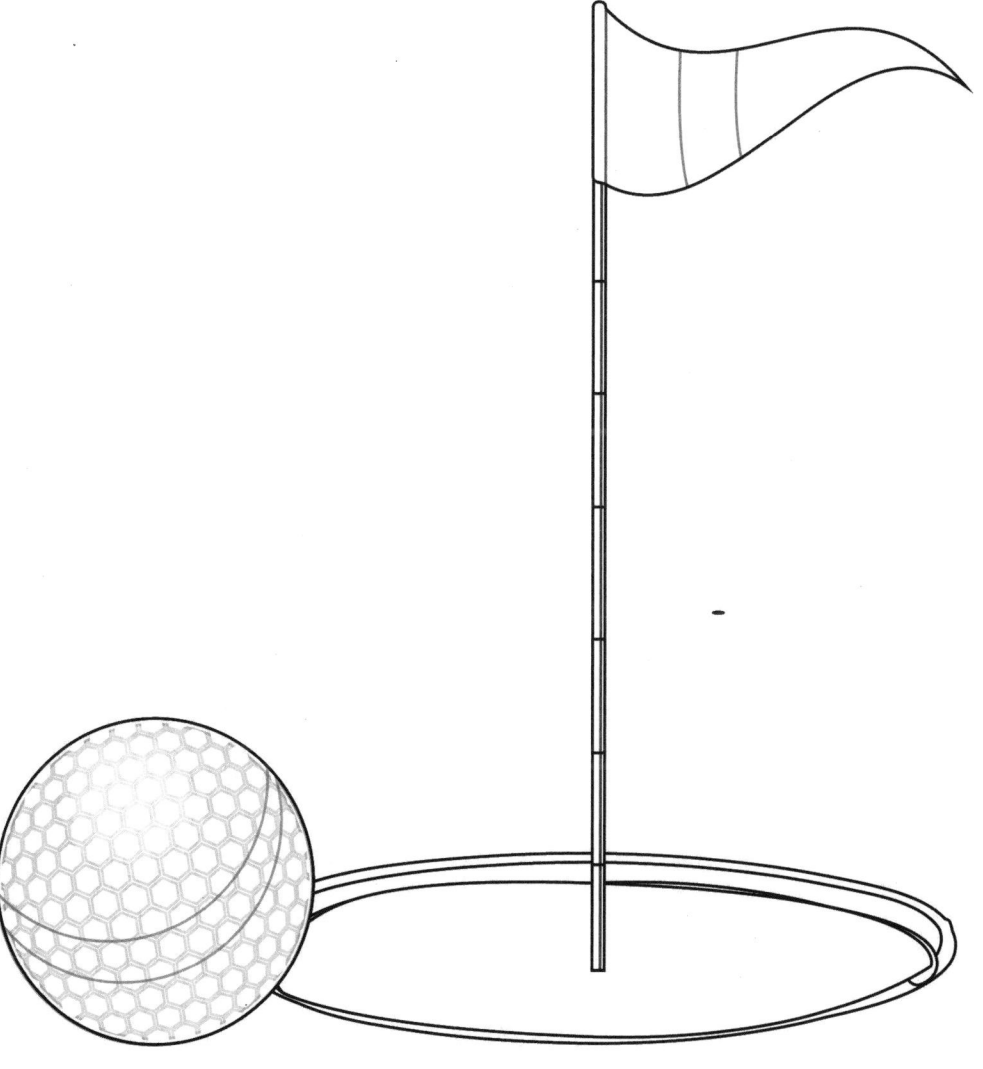

A score that's quite rare

F is for Fairway

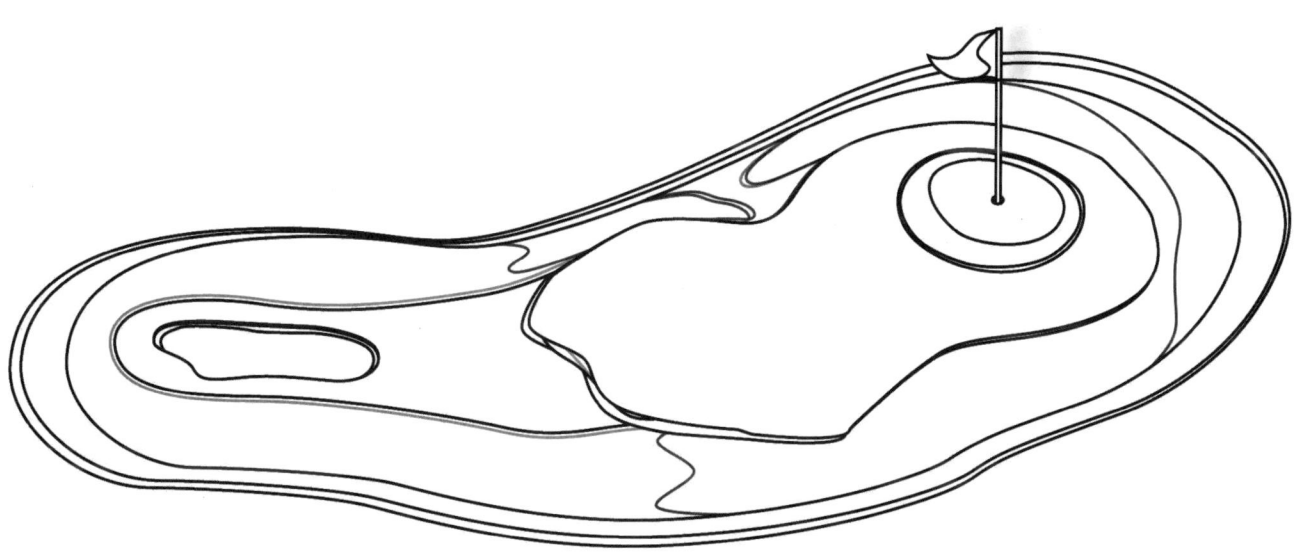

Where the ball should land with care

G is for Green

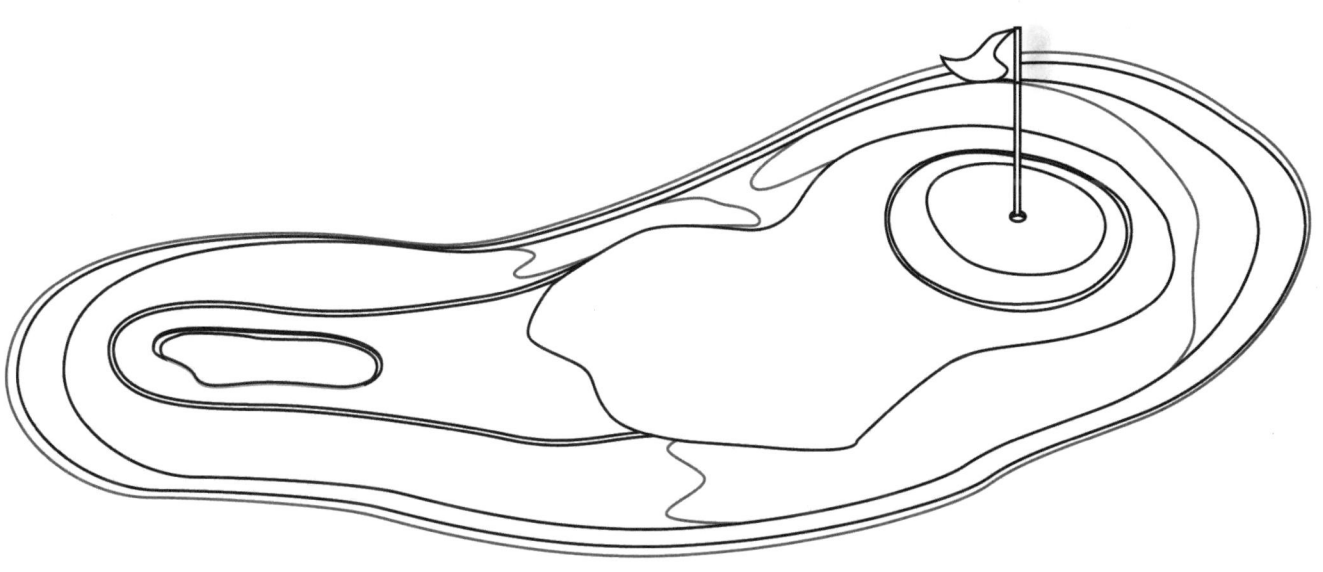

Where the hole can be found

H is for Hole

Where the ball goes round and round

I is for Iron

A club that's so neat

J is for Junior

A young golfer with small feet

K is for Keying

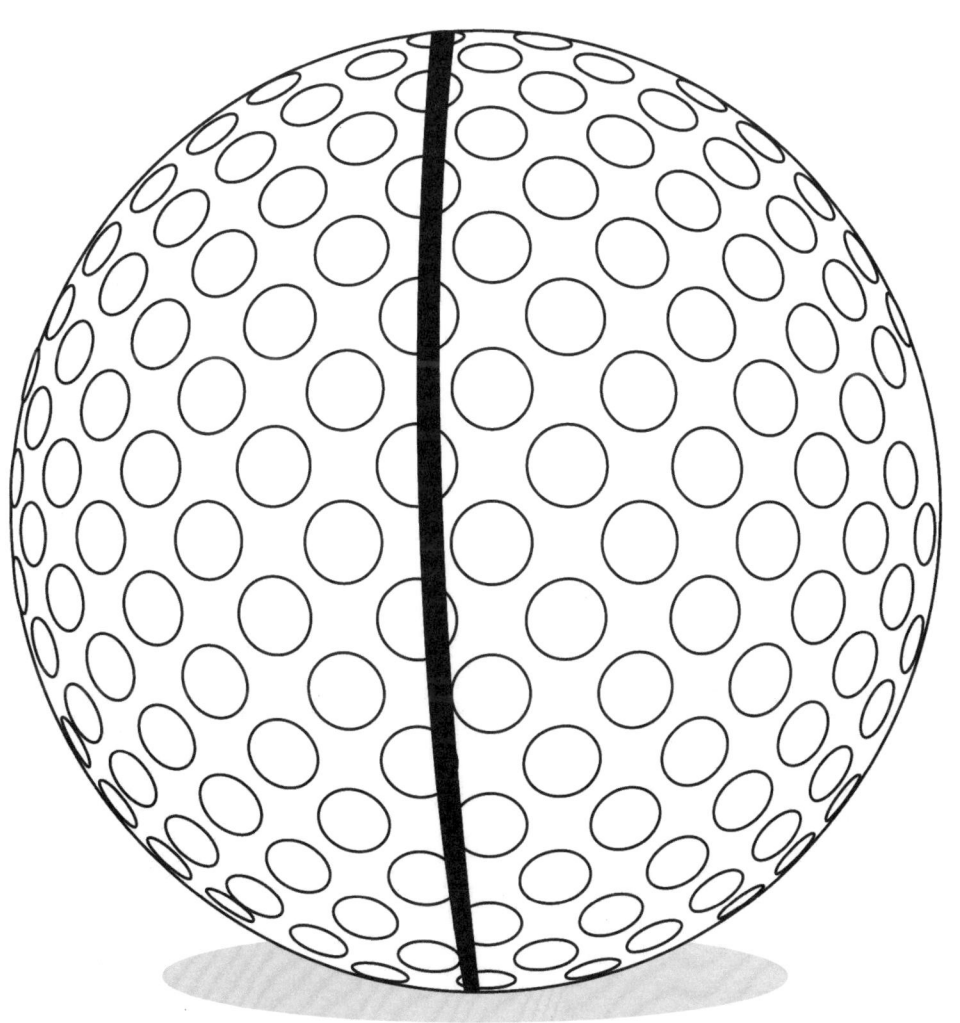

A mark on the ball

L is for Laser

A yardage finder that is small

M is for Mulligan

A do-over, a chance

N is for Nine hole

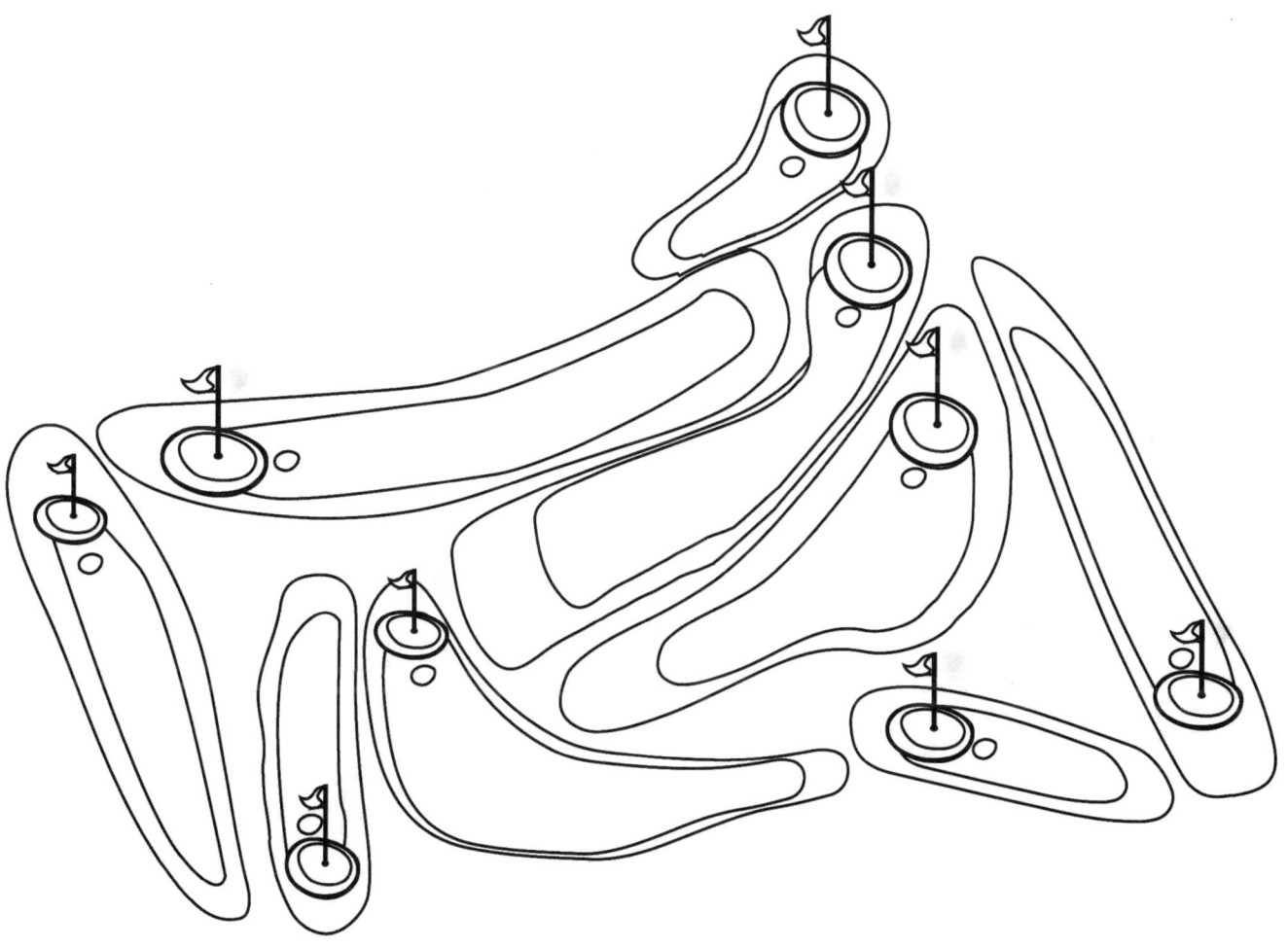

A game that's not a dance

O is for
Out of bounds

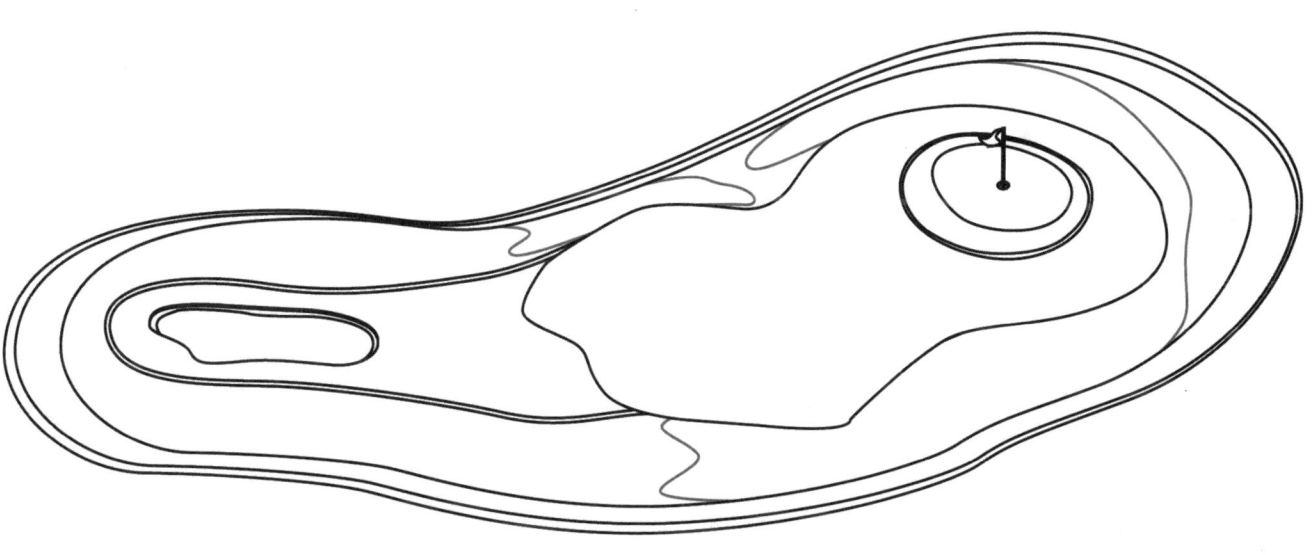

Where the ball can't stay

P is for Putter

With a gentle swing we'll play

Q is for Quail

A bird that we might see

R is for Rough

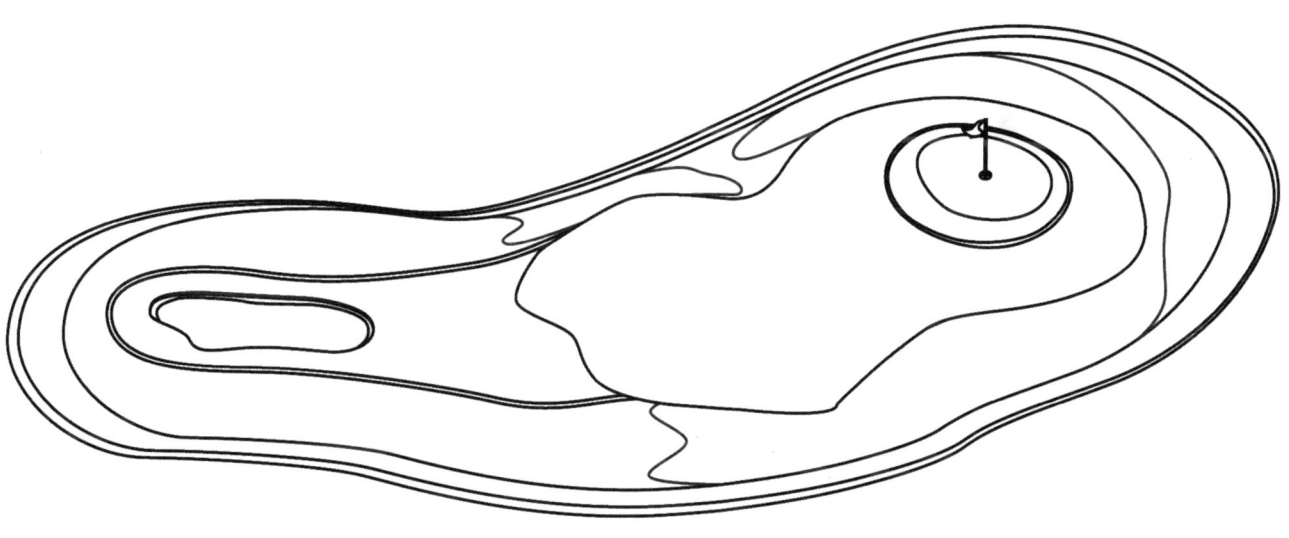

The grass that's wild and free

S is for Sand trap

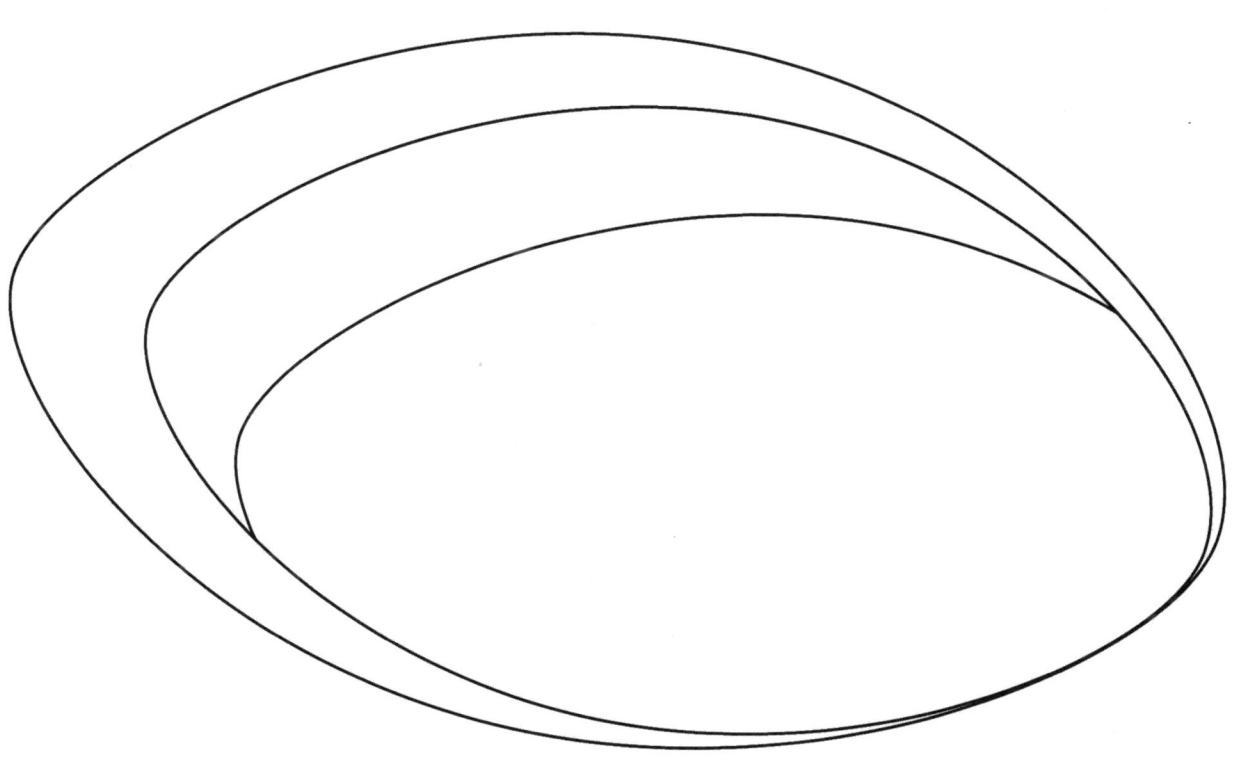

A hazard that's so deep

T is for Tee

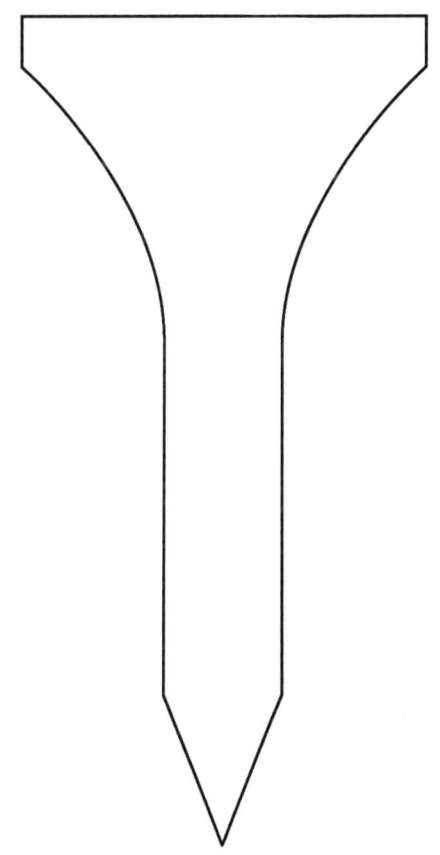

Where our swing will take a leap

U is for Underpar

A score that's really grand

V is for Victory

A feeling that's so planned

W is for Woods

A club that's big and strong,

X is for Extra holes

Where the game goes long.

Y is for Yardage

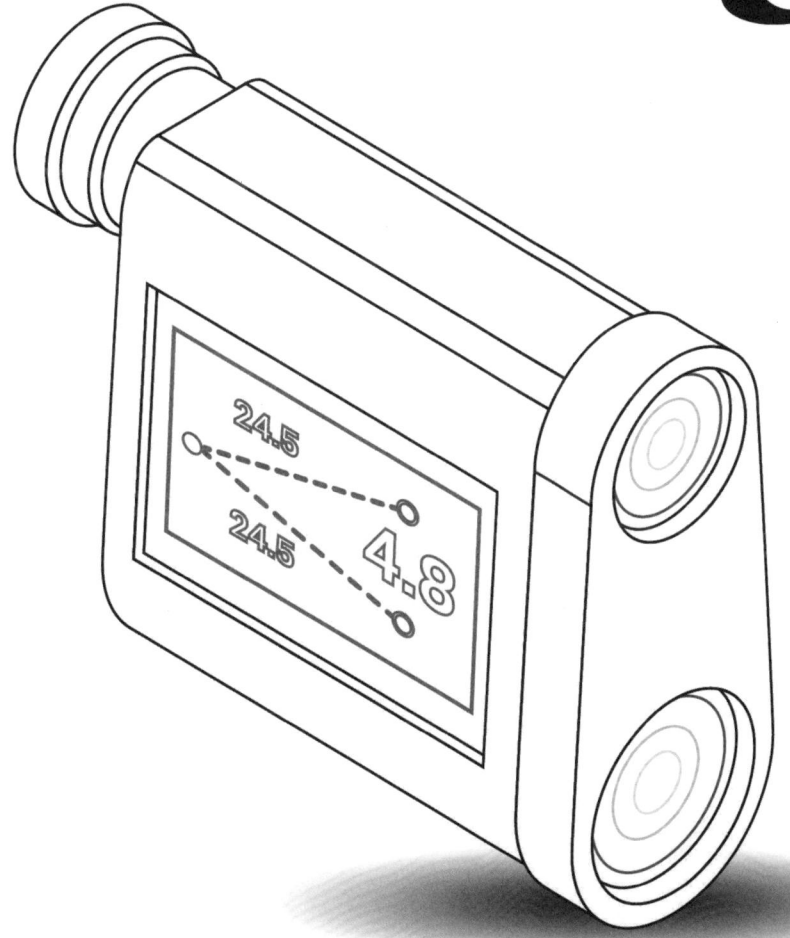

The distance we must gauge,

Z is for Zoom

The speed at which golf cart's blaze.